D0845102

WALTHAM
PUBLIC LIBRARY

Happy

Julie Murray

Abdo
EMOTIONS
Kids

abdopublishing.com

Published by Abdo Kids, a division of ABDO, PO Box 398166, Minneapolis, Minnesota 55439.
Copyright © 2017 by Abdo Consulting Group, Inc. International copyrights reserved in all countries.
No part of this book may be reproduced in any form without written permission from the publisher.

Printed in the United States of America, North Mankato, Minnesota.

052016

092016

 THIS BOOK CONTAINS
RECYCLED MATERIALS

Photo Credits: iStock, Shutterstock

Production Contributors: Teddy Borth, Jennie Forsberg, Grace Hansen

Design Contributors: Candice Keimig, Dorothy Toth

Cataloging-in-Publication Data

Names: Murray, Julie, author.

Title: Happy / by Julie Murray.

Description: Minneapolis, MN : Abdo Kids, [2017] | Series: Emotions | Includes
     bibliographical references and index.

Identifiers: LCCN 2015959084 | ISBN 9781680805239 (lib. bdg.) |
     ISBN 9781680805796 (ebook) | ISBN 9781680806359 (Read-to-me ebook)

Subjects: LCSH: Happiness--Juvenile literature. | Emotions--Juvenile literature.

Classification: DDC 152.4/2--dc23

LC record available at http://lccn.loc.gov/2015959084

Table of Contents

Happy

Being happy feels good.

It is an **emotion**.

Tami is with her sister.

She feels happy.

We smile when we are happy.

Jane is smiling.

9

We laugh when we are happy.

Tom laughs.

Helping others makes us happy.

Ellie helps her grandpa.

Amy plays with her friends.

This makes her happy.

John pets his dog.

This makes him happy.

Charlie is **competitive**.
Playing soccer makes
him happy.

What makes you happy?

Things to Do to Be Happy!

be a good friend

smile and laugh a lot

play with friends

watch a funny movie

Glossary

competitive
having a strong want to win or
be the best.

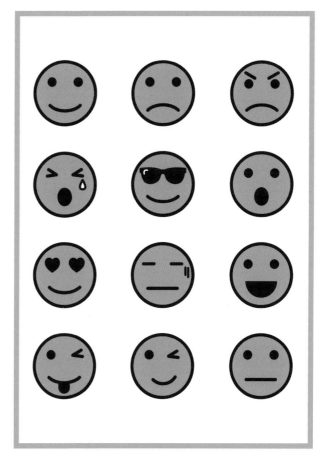

emotion
a strong feeling.

Index

abdokids.com

Use this code to log on to abdokids.com and access crafts, games, videos, and more!

Abdo Kids Code:
EHK5239

WALTHAM
PUBLIC LIBRARY